The Exorcism of My Inner New Yorker: A Memoir of Spirits, Love, and Letting Go

The Exorcism of My Inner New Yorker: A Memoir of Spirits, Love, and Letting Go

Cynthia Barris

10th House Publishers

Published by 10th House Publishers
1733 Route 9
Clifton Park, NY 12065
www.10thhp.com

Cover design by Cynthia Barris

ISBN (Paperback): 9798991233897

Prologue: The Girl Who Lived in Two Worlds

The first time I saw a ghost, I was two years old. He was sitting on our living room couch in Manhattan like he belonged there, wearing a white *guayabera*, smoking a cigar, calm as Sunday. I didn't scream. I didn't run. I just stared. And he stared back, like we both knew something the others didn't.

I didn't tell anyone. Not because I was afraid, but because I already understood that our family could handle loud arguments, louder domino games, and everyone knowing your business. But a toddler medium was pushing it.

The second time I saw a ghost, I was nine. A man appeared dressed like Elvis, or maybe what a Puerto Rican uncle thought Elvis should look like: slick black hair, gold sunglasses, bell-bottoms, too many chains. He smiled and said, "Tell your mother it's Tío Felie."

My mother was in Puerto Rico visiting my grand-parents. When I called and told her, she paused, "How do you know that name?" she asked.

"He told me," I said. "I told you how he looked."

Her voice got small. "That's my godfather. He died before you were born."

"He wants to see you," I told her.

"I'll go to the cemetery," she said.

That evening, I called her again. "Did you go?"

"Yes," she lied. "He shouldn't come back."

But he did. That night he returned, standing at the foot of my bed, wearing the same smile. "Tell her not to lie," he said. "She didn't go."

So I called her back. "Mami, he said you lied. He said you never went. Why did you lie? Please go visit."

Silence. Then, shock. Then, action. She dropped everything and went straight to the cemetery. From that moment on, every time I told her I saw someone, someone not quite here, I saw that look in her eyes. Fear. Not of me exactly, but of what I could see.

That was my introduction to the spirit world. And the beginning of living in two places at once: in the noisy, gritty chaos of Manhattan—and in a quieter place just beyond the veil, where the dead still had things to say.

Dedication

To my mother, who may not have always understood me growing up but never lost hope in me. She never shut me out. Because of her, I learned resilience, patience, and the quiet strength of unconditional support.

To my sons, who showed me a love without limits, a love that expands and endures beyond reason.

To Kevin, who taught me to love fearlessly, to trust without hesitation, and to find safety in the arms of someone who chooses you, again and again, exactly as you are.

And to my family—loud, stubborn, and beautifully imperfect—the roots that held me when I couldn't stand on my own. They taught me that even in chaos, there is shelter. Even in noise, there is belonging.

This is for them.

Introduction: "It Is What It Is"

Life doesn't ask permission to break you. Mine shattered in ways I never saw coming: loss, spirits, Obsessive-compulsive disorder (OCD), and the relentless echo of, "Make us proud." This is the story of how I exorcised the guilt, grief, and noise of my past to find peace in the Rocky Mountains, my kitchen, and the spaces between this world and the next.

Chapter 1: The Call of the City (1976–1985)

ew York City in the '70s was a beautiful disaster. A cracked, chaotic mosaic of cultures, noise, graffiti, and grit. Our neighbors were loud, opinionated, and as permanent as the smell of *sofrito* and King Pine in the hallway.

But even among the living, there were others. Our apartment building had more ghosts than paying tenants. I don't say that as a metaphor; I mean literal ghosts. There was the woman in the stairwell who sang old *boleros* at night—songs full of heartbreak and rue, her voice crackling like a neglected record. Sometimes, if I lingered too long on the steps, I'd catch a scent of cigar smoke and jasmine, though no one was ever there.

Then there was the little boy who played marbles near the mailboxes, the sound of the marbles hitting the wall a whisper against the hum of the flickering hallway lights. He'd glance up when I passed, his dark eyes holding a question he never spoke. If I got too close, his form would dissolve like smoke, the marbles rolling away on their own, as if pulled by invisible hands.

And the shadow figure- tall, shapeless, standing in the bathroom doorway every night while I brushed my teeth. It never moved, never spoke, just watched from the threshold, its presence a cold weight against my spine.

None of them spoke to me. Not in words, at least. But sometimes, in the silence, I felt their confusion pressing in, the quiet, restless bewilderment of spirits who didn't quite understand why they were here. Or worse, why I could see them. I started muttering, "Leave me alone," under my breath, more out of habit than expectation. They never listened. They never reacted. They just stared, as if I were the ghost, and they were waiting for me to finally explain myself.

I got used to them. That's what you do in New York: you get used to things. You get used to sirens lulling you to sleep. To steam pipes hissing like angry cats. To doormen who knew everyone's business, and grandmothers who pretended not to. You get used to feeling like the whole world lives in your building, and that not all of them are still alive.

I never felt afraid. Curious, yes. Annoyed, sometimes. But afraid? No, not of spirits, anyway. I was more afraid of Mami catching me sneaking snacks after bedtime.

We were Puerto Rican and proud—loud music, louder family, and a faith that was equal parts Catholicism, superstition, and whispered stories. Nobody ever sat me down and said, "We believe in spirits." But they believed in signs, in dreams, and in gut feelings that couldn't be ignored. And so did I.

I didn't have the words for it then, but I was starting to realize that I straddled two worlds: the one everyone else could see, and the one that hovered just behind it. I learned early on that the living talk over each other, but the dead wait for you to listen.

The city was my first church—a place of saints and shadows, where spirits crowded the *bodegas* and my family's pride weighed more than the subway cars beneath our feet.

Chapter 2: Meet My Family: The Party People

Before you understand anything about me, you need to meet my family. Because in the Barris household, nothing was ever just a moment—it was a production. Every birthday was a festival. Every dinner, a declaration of love served with a side of passive aggression. And every holiday was a Macy's Thanksgiving Day Parade—but with more Corona and Heineken and louder yelling.

We didn't just celebrate—we *survived* each other.

My Family Survival Guide:
- Never let the Coquito run out.
- If someone brings up politics, distract them with *pernil* (roasted pork) and *arroz con gandules*.
- Your business is everyone's business—but deny everything.

We were loud, messy, fiercely loyal, and emotionally fluent in two languages: Spanish and side-eye. Every argument was just another way of saying, "I love you, but you're being ridiculous." And every family gathering guaranteed three things: food, drama, and music—usually in that order.

Mami (Lucy):

My mother is the human version of *café con leche*—sweet, comforting, and liable to scald you if you're not paying attention. She could love you so hard it left a mark, and she believed in being honest, even when it hurt, especially when it hurt. She taught me how to fight for what I believe in and how to cry without ruining my mascara. She also taught me that silence can be a weapon, and forgiveness a revolution.

Growing up, my mother was my constant. She never left my side, even when she didn't understand the world I inhabited. She knew I had a gift—one she couldn't interpret and frightened her. She couldn't tell me which spirit was good or bad, couldn't explain why I saw what others didn't.

Raised in a devout home, she was taught to pray, to trust in miracles—but spirits and premonitions she feared as they were the devil's work. Yet she never turned away. She never called me a liar. Instead, she'd say, "Cindy, please don't tell me . . . unless it's really bad and we need to know." She didn't shut me down; she just didn't know how to navigate the unknown. Her fear was real, but so was her love. And in the end, that was enough.

Papi (Victor):

My father didn't need to raise his voice to command a room. He had that quiet strength, that look that said, *"Don't play with me, but I love you more than I'll ever say out loud."* He wasn't perfect, but he was real. He taught me how to spot liars, how to never hold back, and how to always—*always*—show up for the people you love. He smelled like cologne, and whenever he hugged me, I felt like the world couldn't touch me.

Growing up, my dad was my anchor. He didn't just tell me to be strong; he made me believe I already was. "Don't waste time on what people say about you," he'd grumble. "They don't live your life." And unlike others, he never dismissed my gift. He understood it in a way my mother couldn't, because his mother had carried it too. He wasn't a stranger to the unseen.

Working as a caretaker at the museum, he'd joke about the spirits rearranging chairs and playing the piano when no one was looking. He grew up between worlds: the one we all shared and the one his mother navigated. He never claimed to see what she saw, but he'd yell into empty rooms when chairs slid across the floors, demanding the shadows "Stop their damn nonsense."

Still, he'd made a promise to my mother—to keep me away from the darker side of the gift. So when I asked questions, the answers were sealed tight. Their silence left me adrift, wondering if I was just imaging it all.

This is when my OCD started to kick in, I had to have everything in its place, it was the only thing I had control over. As a child, I set my Barbies and dolls a certain way, and no one was allowed to move it. I knew if someone had been in my room as I would spot the one thing that was moved. With a glance, I knew when something was out of place. I had no control over the spirits, but I had control over my OCD.

Once, my father sighed and said, "We'll explain when you're older." But older never came. Grandma passed before she could teach me, and Dad, tight-lipped as ever, took his stories with him. Now, I miss him most when the house is too quiet and when the spirits come looking for someone. I wish he were still here to tell them, "Not tonight."

Uncle Jr.:

My mother's younger brother cooked like he was feeding a nation at war. His pork shoulder (*pernil*) could've brokered peace treaties or started revolutions, depending on how long it had bathed in marinade. The man spoke sparingly, but when he did, even the loudmouth *tíos* stopped mid-sentence to listen.

Family chaos rolled off him like water on a hot skillet. While the rest of us ricocheted between arguments and silent treatments, Uncle Jr. moved through the house like a gentle hurricane—calming winds, steady pressure. "Why fight when you can eat?" he'd murmur, already herding us toward the kitchen with those knowing eyes.

His magic trick? That voice—smooth as *café con leche*, and warm as fresh Puerto Rican bread. When he said "*ve a la cocina*," you went, not because he commanded it, but because you knew whatever waited on those ceramic plates would taste like love made tangible.

Even now, I measure peace by the scent of his *sofrito*—onion, garlic, and quiet understanding simmering in equal parts

Títi Mayra:

Tío Junior's other half—his beginning and his always. They met in school, two kids with no idea they were writing their first chapter at fourteen. While other childhood romantics fizzled out, theirs simmered, then boiled over into a love that lasted decades.

Mayra didn't walk through life—she danced. Hips swaying to merengue in the supermarket aisle, fingers snapping to salsa while stirring *arroz con gandules (rice with pigeon peas)*, bare feet tracing bachata steps on the tiled floor at midnight.

Her laughter could shake pictures off walls, her hugs left traces of perfume and fried plantains on your clothes.

She lived unapologetically, loudly, as if secrets were a waste of good sunlight. Maybe her joy came easy because she'd found her soulmate young—or maybe she just decided early on that happiness wasn't something you found, but something you cooked up daily, like her famous *sancocho (Caribbean stew)*: everything thrown in, all flavors melting together, better with time.

Even now, when I hear a trumpet's bright punch or catch a whiff of ripe plantains, I see them— Junior at the stove, Mayra stealing a taste over his shoulder, her gold bangles clinking like wind chimes in a storm.

Cousin Normalys:

The miracle child of Tío Junior and Títi Mayra— my little cousin who called me *bruja* like it was a crown, not a curse. Where others whispered about my gifts, she proclaimed them. "You don't just see ghosts," she'd say, adjusting the lens on her camera, "you translate them."

She was sixteen going on sixty, with a soul that remembered too much and a laugh that made you forget. We bonded over grainy film shots of old family pictures.

"Your problem," she told me once, saltwater drying in her wavy hair after a midnight scream session at Seaside Heights, "is you keep waiting for healing to look pretty. But sometimes it's snot and tears in the Atlantic at 3 AM or it's a spirit photobombing your shot with their unfinished business." She tossed a seashell at my chest. "So give them a damn filter and keep shooting." I finally understood: magic isn't about fixing broken things. It's about framing them so the cracks catch the light.

Títi Millie:

My mother's sister—some swore they were twins. These two moved through life like a single soul split between two bodies. No matter the state, no matter the city, they always found a way to plant their homes within walking distance, as if the umbilical cord had never been cut.

Every Saturday, like clockwork, the entire family migrated to Titi Millie's house. The front door might as well have been a revolving one—she fed everyone who crossed her threshold, whether they were hungry or not. Just like Abuela, who'd have fed the entire block if given half a chance. Midnight or midday, the moment your foot touched her white tiled floors, she'd already be halfway to the stove, asking, "*¿Tú comiste?*" as if the very idea of you going unfed was a personal offense.

But more than her cooking, it was her listening that nourished us. When family dramas reached hurricane decibels, Títi Millie was the eye of the storm—calm, steady, absorbing the chaos without judgment. She had this quiet magic of pulling clarity from your tangled words, of making you feel understood before you even understood yourself.

In her presence, the world softened. No wonder Dinelia inherited that gift—the same patient silence, the same knowing nods, the same ability to make a fractured heart feel whole.

Some houses are made of bricks; Títi Millie's was built of warm plates and warmer embraces—a sanctuary where no one ever left empty, neither in stomach nor in soul.

Uncle Ralph:

Uncle Ralph, my uncle by marriage on my mother's side, cooked with patience. He was the quiet observer in a family of loud personalities, but when he spoke, you listened. He always had a story, a proverb, or a joke that made you laugh so hard your stomach hurt.

When he arrived from Puerto Rico to work with my father, I was sixteen and starving for someone who wouldn't flinch when I spoke of spirits. He didn't just believe me—he understood. "*Yo tambien*," he'd say, tapping his temple.

He confessed his own premonitions, how dreams would slip into his sleep like uninvited prophecies, and how he'd wake *knowing they'd* come to pass. He didn't claim to grasp the full weight of his gift, but he respected the unknown with a humility that calmed the chaos in me. Uncle Ralph hugged you with both arms and made you feel like everything would be okay. Uncle Ralph taught me how to peel a green plantain without losing my mind and how to spot a liar without saying a word. He was a vault of family history, a protector of traditions, and someone who knew when I needed comfort, even when I didn't.

Cousin Dinelia:

My cousin, my anchor. We were more sisters than cousins, connected by blood and bonded by something deeper. Dinelia was the one person I never had to explain myself to. When the world spun too fast, Dinelia was the one who grabbed my hand and reminded me to breathe. We grew up tangled together, our mothers were attached at the hip one would say. Two veins from the same root. Though younger, she had an old soul's wisdom, a way of speaking that cut through the noise in my head.

I told her everything—the spirits that lingered at the edges of my vision, the heartbreaks that left me raw, the relentless pull of my OCD that made me rearrange the world to feel in control. She taught me to redirect the twitches, the compulsions, into creation. "If you need things to move, move them where it matters." That's how baking became my sanctuary—the measured cups, the rhythmic kneading, the alchemy of chaos into something sweet. It wasn't a cure, but a truce. We cried, we laughed until our stomachs ached. She stood beside me when the spirits whispered too loud and when the world felt too heavy. Through every unraveling, she was there. Not to fix me, but to remind me I was never broken.

My Cousin Billie Jo:

My brother from another mother. Billie Jo is the kind of cousin who doesn't beat around the bush, he says what he means. Even if it's a question that cuts straight to your soul, he never skirts around the truth. Billie Jo didn't flinch when I talked about seeing spirits. He leaned in closer. He's the cousin who holds space for the messy parts of life—who taught me that vulnerability isn't weakness, it's survival.

His honesty? Sacred. His love? Unshakable.

I had the honor of naming him when we were kids, after my favorite singer in the '80s—Billy Joel. (Though he'd tease, "You spelled it wrong, but I'll allow it.") And just like his namesake's songs, Billie

Jo became the soundtrack to my life's wild, beautiful, imperfect journey.

We weren't perfect, we were far from it, but we were ours. Family is complicated. I have half-siblings. I am the youngest, yet as my father's illness tightened its grip, we unraveled. Strangers now, where there was once shared laughter, shared secrets. Not the ending anyone hopes for, but reality.

This is how I begin: With my family. A family of storytellers, secret-keepers, and spirit-sensitives—whether they admitted it or not. Growing up among them meant I learned early on how to read the room, how to throw a *chancla* with precision, and how to love without condition.

And maybe most importantly, I learned how to stand in the fire without getting burned.

Outside of my family, I had friends who knew my secret—who listened without judgment when I spoke of the things I couldn't explain.

One evening after visiting my family, I met up with a friend and confessed how, whenever I shared messages people weren't expecting, their first reaction was to call me crazy.

She just smiled, crunching on a cheese doodle, and said, *"You're not crazy, you're just tuned into a station most people pretend doesn't exist."*

We were lying on a rooftop in Brooklyn, passing that bag of bright orange snacks back and forth like it was holy communion. The city hummed below us, a distant symphony of car horns and laughter, but up there, it was just us and the stars. She believed in me before I ever did, and on nights when the world felt too loud, I'd think back to that moment— the cool concrete beneath us, the sky stretched wide and endless, our voices tangled together as we laughed about ghosts and boys and everything in between.

"Being called crazy is just the price of seeing the truth," she once told me. And maybe she was right. Maybe the truth wasn't meant to be easy. Maybe it was supposed to rattle cages, to make people uncomfortable. But in that moment, with her beside me, it didn't feel like a burden. It felt like a secret worth keeping.

Chapter 3: Embracing My Gift (And Why I Tried to Return It.)

People think that having a gift means you're lucky. That it's glamorous or exciting, like you walk around whispering secrets from beyond and charging $50 a reading. But let me tell you something: when spirits show up at 3 a.m. and you've got school the next morning, it's not *glamorous*, it's exhausting.

Everything came to light when I was thirteen when I saw my grandmother in her coffin. The weird part? She wasn't dead yet. I remember the vision as if it were happening right in front of me. Her hair was brushed back just the way she liked it. She was wearing the pale pink dress she wore to Easter Mass the year before. Her hands were folded, her eyes closed, and there were fresh white lilies all around.

I ran to her the next morning. "Abuela," I said, shaking, "I saw you in a coffin." She didn't even flinch. Instead of fear, she took my hand gently in hers and said, "I know, *mi amor*. I'm ready." Confusion twisted in my gut. "But why did I see it if you're still here?" Her grip tightened, surprising me with its strength. "Because you have the gift," she said. "Use it for good. Don't do what I did." There was guilt in those words. A warning. "Don't be afraid," she said. "Spirits talk to you because you *listen.* The living are the ones who need help hearing."

I nodded, pretending to be brave. But inside, I wanted to give the gift back. I didn't want to see dead people. I didn't want to feel things I couldn't explain or hear voices no one else could. But it didn't stop.

Later, I'd learn the truth: my grandmother had been forbidden from speaking to me about the gift. My parents, terrified of what they didn't understand, had made her promise. "She's too young," they argued. "What if she learns to twist it? To use it like—" They never finished the sentence, but I knew. Like Abuela had.

Rumors slithered through our family about her past-whispers of bad juju, of fortunes told for the right price, of hexes slipped into a rival's coffee. My parents feared the gift wasn't just sight-it was influenced. And they were desperate to believe that if they didn't name it, it couldn't take root in me.

So they buried it in silence. But gifts like ours don't stay buried. They push through the soil like stubborn weeds, cracking the foundation of every "don't ask, don't tell" rule meant to contain them.

Abuela died three days after our conversation. At her funeral, I recognized every detail-the wilted roses, the way the light cut through the stained-glass saints, the weight of my father's hand on my shoulder, shaking. Just as I'd seen. That was the first time I understood: the gift wasn't just visions. It was a legacy. And I had to choose whether to carry it or let it drag me under.

A year later, I told my mother to call my aunt. The scent hit me first-that sharp, woody cologne my cousin always wore too much of. It flooded my nostrils, thick as smoke, though no one had entered the room. My skin prickled. The air tasted like a warning.

"Something's wrong," I said. "I smell cologne." Mami froze mid-motion, a spoon hovering over her café con leche. She looked at me like I'd grown a second head. "It's strong," I said. "Like someone just walked through here." The phantom scent clung to my clothes, my hair. I could almost see the imprint of him standing in our kitchen grinning, alive, not yet gone.

She called, reluctantly. The way you humor a child telling ghost stories. The wait that came through the phone was answer enough. My cousin had passed away that morning.

After that, Mami stopped questioning what I felt. She'd hear my warnings-check on Abuelo, don't let Papi drive today, She accepted what was to come. But she didn't embrace it, either. She feared it. And maybe a part of me did, too. Because knowing someone was gone before the phone rang? That hollow click of fate settling into place? Feeling a cold hand brush your shoulder in an empty room—

no pressure, just a whisper of fingertips and the certainty you're not alone? Smelling someone's perfume on the anniversary of their death? It's not something you get used to, but I learned how to.

I learned how to ground myself when the room became too crowded with things I couldn't see. The air would thicken first—a pressure against my temples, a static hum in my molars. Then the shadows would deepen, not with absence, but with presence. A breath where there shouldn't be one. The weight of eyes on my back. At first, I'd freeze. Let them press in until my own heartbeat defends me. But slowly, I learned. Salt under the tongue to mute their whispers. Cold water on my wrist shocks me back into my body. I taught myself to exhale in a slow, steady stream, pushing them out with my breath like smoke. Not now, I'd think, and if that didn't work, I'd snap my fingers once—sharp as a bone breaking—to sever the connection.

I learned how to protect my energy, how to say, "Not now," without saying a word.

I started meditating, not the serene, candlelit kind you see in movies, but something messier-knees dug into my bedroom floor, chanting "I am here, you are there" until the words lost meaning and became a wall. The shower became sacred. Under scalding water, I'd recite affirmations like armor: "Nothing crosses without permission." Steam filled my lungs, and for those few minutes, I was untouchable.

Walking to school, I'd murmur mantras under my breath, syncing them to my footsteps. "My body is mine. My mind is mine." The dead could walk beside me, but they couldn't hitch a ride.

And I learned that being a medium didn't mean being in the middle—it meant *holding space* between worlds.

It meant being the bridge, but I was still a kid. I didn't want to be a bridge; I wanted to be normal. I didn't know yet—normal wasn't coming for me.

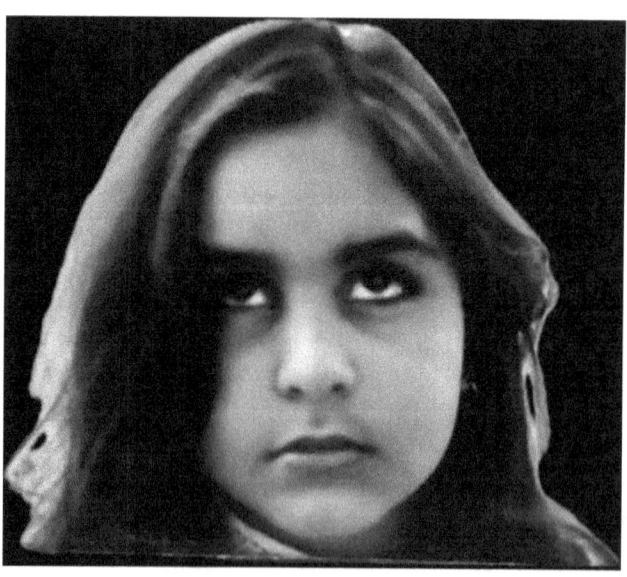

Chapter 4: The Weight of Expectations

Growing up in a Puerto Rican family in New York came with its own user manual. Not a printed one, of course. Ours was unwritten but deeply ingrained—passed down through looks, tones of voice, and the subtle art of guilt. There was also a checklist. It wasn't official, but trust me, it was real.

My Family's Checklist for Success:
- √ Become a doctor (I got as far as medical billing)
- √ Marry a nice Puerto Rican boy (I married a white guy named Kevin)
- √ Have babics (this one... still stings)

From a young age, I knew what was expected of me: be smart but not *too* outspoken, be helpful but not *too* independent, and be strong but never show pain. In our family, tears were private, pride was public, and shame—well, shame was a family event.

I was good at following the rules—at first. I got the grades, said *bendición* to every adult in the room, and learned how to carry the weight of everyone's hopes on my back like a pro. But even back then, I knew I was different. Not just because I saw spirits, but because I *felt* everything more deeply. Every joy, every loss, and every disappointment. Mine and everyone else's.

School was its own kind of haunting. I could read upside down, decipher scrambled words like they were written clearly, but the multiplication tables might as well have been hieroglyphics. My mother's flashcards became our nightly ritual of frustration, "Cynthia, 3×3=9. 3×2=6. Now what's 3×3?" Her voice was tight with forced patience as my tears smudged the numbers. Yet I could recall every address, every phone number like digits raining from the sky.

The disappointment in my parents' eyes cut deeper than any failing grade. College graduates, both—what would they do with a daughter who couldn't conquer basic arithmetic? In our world, "learning disability" sounded too much like "dead end."

I don't remember exactly when the shift came, only that after Abuela passed, something in me settled. Maybe it was her last words—"You have a gift, Míja"—that finally untangled the knots in my brain. Suddenly, I could strategize my way to Monopoly victories against my cousins. Architecture's precise lines, biology's intricate systems, chemistry's elegant equations—where numbers had been fog, these subjects were clear water.

Was it magic? Grief? Or simply being seen for the first time? I still don't know. But the girl who cried over flashcards became the woman who could focus with razor intensity.

When I didn't check off the boxes in the right order, the questions started. "Cynthia, why didn't you become a nurse like your Aunt?" "Still no children? What are you waiting for?" "Why'd you marry a gringo?"

No one ever said, *"I'm proud of you for surviving."* Or *"You're brave for choosing your own path."* No. Pride was conditional. Love was unquestionable— but pride? That had a dress code and a deadline.

The truth is, I wanted all the things they wanted for me. I did. I wanted to be a mother. I wanted to feel like I belonged to a life that made sense to everyone else. But that wasn't the life I got. I got something messier, quieter, and—for a long time— lonelier.

The Breaking Point:

There's a special kind of grief in not becoming a daughter your mother imagined while rocking you to sleep. It lives in the space between her hopeful prayers and your quiet rebellions-a phantom child whose shadow grows longer with every choice that takes you further from their dreams. And beneath it all, the shame burns slow and constant: how dare you ache for a life you willingly turned away from?

For years, I wore my loneliness like a second skin. When the pressure built until my vision blurred, when the weight of everyone's disappointment pressed down until I gasped for air between sobs, I'd wait until the house was asleep. The shower became my confessional-scalding water erasing tears, my cries muffled by the roar of the pipes. I'd emerge raw and pink, my sorrows dissolving down the drain with the suds.

Then came Dinelia.

She cornered me after a Saturday dinner, her grip firm on my arm as she steered me into her bedroom. "Cynthia," she said, turning me to face her. Her thumbs rubbed circles on the inside of my wrists, and she looked straight into my eyes. "Talk to me. This silence is eating you alive."

I collapsed onto the edge of her bed, the springs creaking under the weight of all I'd carried. And then, like a dam breaking, it all came rushing out. The years of swallowing my truth. The crushing guilt of choosing myself. The terrifying freedom of being loved for who I was, not who I was supposed to be.

Tears tracked hot down my face as I confessed things I'd never dared speak aloud-how I both cherished and resented my parents' dreams for me. Dinelia's own tears fell silently as she listened. When my voice finally gave out, she stood abruptly and pulled me into an embrace so fierce it lifted me off my feet. Her arms wrapped around me like a life preserver, her cheek pressed wet against mine. In that moment, I felt something shift-as if she was absorbing some of my sorrow through her skin.

She never offered empty platitudes. Never told me it would be okay. Just held me until my breathing slowed to match hers, until the weight in my chest lightened from a boulder to a stone. And when we emerged, eyes swollen and hands still clasped, she sealed our pact with a look. Not a word of that afternoon would ever pass her lips. Some truths are too sacred to share. Some healing only happens in the quiet spaces between two hearts that remember you before the world told you who to be.

There's a grief in not fulfilling the version of you your family dreamed of. And there's shame in grieving a life you never had.

But here's what they didn't teach us growing up: You don't owe anyone your suffering. And you're allowed to rewrite the checklist.

Now, mine looks more like this:
- Find peace
- Speak the/your Truth
- Love deeply—even if it looks different
- Bake when anxious
- Listen to the dead, but live for the living. I'll admit there are still days I want my family's

approval like air. But these days, I breathe for myself first.

Mom and I on the subway escalators

Chapter 5: OCD – The Control Freak

emory ***Age five, clutching my mother's hand on the subway, counting tiles to calm my racing heart. Obsessive-compulsive disorder (OCD) wasn't a diagnosis yet—just "Cynthia's quirks."

Let me tell you something about living between two worlds: the spiritual one doesn't come with labels or logic. So, the one thing I could control— *everything else.*

My brain has two settings:
1. Everything must be in its place right **now**.
2. Why isn't everything in its place right **NOW**?

Some people see dust, I see betrayal. Some people walk into a messy room and think, *It's fine.* I walk in and think, *This is why the spirits won't leave.*

OCD isn't about being "a little neat," it's about order being the only thing between you and chaos. It's about lining up your shoes not because you want to—but because if you *don't*, you can feel something unraveling, something deep and unnamable. It's about keeping your world stitched together when the seams are always threatening to burst.

OCD Ritual: Rearranging the spice rack at 3 a.m. Alphabetized. Always.

Confession:

I once reorganized a stranger's grocery cart at Stop & Shop because the cereal was fraternizing with the frozen peas. I didn't say a word—just gently moved the Raisin Bran away from the bag of tater tots and gave her a polite smile like, *You're welcome.*

In a life where spirits appear without warning, grief knocks the wind out of you, and dreams don't go according to plan, *control* became my coping mechanism. My armor. My invisible leash on a world I could never fully predict.

But here's the catch: OCD isn't cute; it's mentally and physically exhausting. You can't shut your brain off. You're trapped in a loop of "Did I leave something out of place? Is everything where it should be?" Because if it isn't, your body reacts before your mind can reason; twitching, itching, like ants crawling under your skin. The wrong angle of the picture frame, a chair pulled slightly too far from the table—small things that shouldn't matter but do—violently.

For me, peace only comes when everything is untouched, undisturbed. Even when no one else has been home, I check. And recheck. And recheck again. Simple tasks become battles; rest feels like a gamble. There's always that voice: If you relax, something bad will happen. Logically, I know it's a lie. But OCD doesn't care about logic. It's part of me that negotiates with ghosts, and it's not taking any chances.

And yet, there's a strange peace in knowing your patterns, in finding clarity in your compulsions. My rituals gave me rhythm. They gave me the illusion of safety—and sometimes that illusion was enough to get me through the day.

Therapy helped a little, so did Kevin (more on him later). But what helped most of all was the slow, brutal lesson that control and peace weren't the same thing. I learned it through trial and error—through rituals that left me exhausted and a mind that still wouldn't quiet. Then, one day, it hit me like a gut punch: I have control. So why am I still on edge?

That was the moment I realized the truth. Control wasn't peace. Control was a clenched fist, a locked door, a breath held too long. Peace was letting go. And OCD had spent years convincing me that was the one thing I could never do.

Chapter 6: The Loss of My Boys

Motherhood wasn't a dream—it was a primal need. When I lost my sons, grief didn't come in stages. It was a free-fall. I stopped baking. Stopped taking photos. Stopped believing in a God who'd take them.

No one teaches you how to grieve the children you never got to raise. They don't send you home from the hospital with instructions on how to breathe through silence, or how to fold baby clothes you never got to use, or how to answer the question, *"Do you have kids?"* without swallowing glass.

A miscarriage is the kind of heartbreak that lives in your bones. It doesn't matter how far along you were, or how long you held them in your arms—or if you ever got to at all. What matters is that in your heart, you were already a mother. And then you weren't.

I lost my boys before the world ever knew their names.

No one had time to plan a shower, but I had dreams. I had morning sickness. I had hope. And when it ended, I had nothing but a body that felt like it had failed, and a heart that couldn't figure out how to keep beating the same way.

Grief isn't a storm you weather; it's not something that passes. It's learning how to live in the rain. How to get up every morning knowing someone is missing and love the world anyway.

For a long time, I didn't think I'd recover. Not really. I walked around holding space for ghosts who never even took their first breath.

Then came Alani.

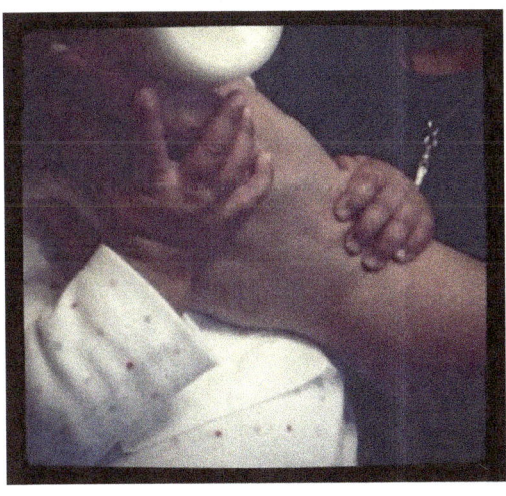

Three years after losing my boys, my niece was born. The first time I held her, something inside me cracked and bloomed at the same time. She was tiny and soft and new to the world—and when her fingers curled around mine, I felt my heart shift. Her breath was warm against my collarbone, her weight light but anchoring, and for the first time in what felt like forever, I felt whole. Not fixed. Not healed. But whole, in a new way.

Because love isn't pie, you don't run out. Losing some doesn't mean there's less to give, it just means you love differently—with more tenderness, with more fear, with more reverence.

I still think about them—my boys. Sometimes when I light a candle, the flame flickers just a little too perfectly. Sometimes I dream about little feet running across wooden floors. Sometimes I just *feel* them—like soft whispers in the background of my life.

I never stopped being their mother; I just had to learn how to mother them in their absence. And to forgive my body, my grief, and the silence that followed.

Chapter 7: Conversations with the Past

People think being a medium means you get closure. That the dead line up neatly like they're waiting at the DMV, take a number, say their peace, and move on.

Let me clear that up: *they don't.*

The dead come when they want, say what they want, and sometimes just . . . linger. Not because they're malevolent or lost—though some are—but because *we* are. Mediums aren't magicians. We don't summon healing with a chant and sage. We're bridges. Messy, human bridges who are still dealing with our own unfinished business.

Especially when it comes to family. Especially when it comes to *Papi.* He died before we had a final conversation. Not the "I love you" kind—I said that, many times. But the *real* kind. The one where I got to ask him why he never said he was proud, why he always spoke fondly of my brother and not me. Why he kept secrets and wasn't honest with me?

In my family, when it comes to the men, it's always hard to get them to open up about feelings—especially the ones born in my dad's era. He was always guarded, and perhaps he had no issue speaking fondly of my brother because he was the only boy. My father was never a sentimental person. He was tough, rough around the edges, but you knew he loved you through his actions.

Still, I wish I could have asked him. I wish I could have cracked open that hardened shell just once, not for an apology or some grand revelation, but just to understand. To know if he ever saw himself in me. If his silence was disappointment or just the only language he knew.

He visits me sometimes, but not often. When he does, he's usually quiet. He stands in the corner and doesn't say much. Once I asked him, "Are you proud of me?"

He just looked at me with that same half-smile I remember from childhood—like he was about to tell a joke, or cry. I woke up before he could answer.

That's the thing about the dead. They don't always give you what you want. But sometimes they give you what you *need*.

I bring blue flowers to his grave every year— hydrangeas if I can find them. Blue was his favorite color. I don't know if he knew that I knew. But I did and still do.

This letter won't resolve what was left unsaid. It won't hand me closure like a neatly wrapped box. But writing to him—pressing these words into silence—brings me a kind of peace. At least now, after all these years, I've said what I could never say when he was here.

Letter to Papi:

I hope I made you proud. And if not, I hope you like the flowers I bring to your grave. They're blue— your favorite.
I forgive you. For everything.
I hope you've forgiven me too—for needing more than you could give.

Some conversations never finish. Some don't even begin. But if there's one thing I've learned from the dead, it's this: *Love is louder than silence. And forgiveness is its own kind of mediumship.*

Chapter 8: Finding Love Again

Let's get one thing straight—I wasn't looking for love. Not after everything I had endured and survived. Not after the loss, the grief, the divorce, the late-night conversations with the dead, and the deafening silence that followed. Love felt like something reserved for other people. People without baggage. People without ghosts.

And then came Kevin.

I met him on an old dating website I'd forgotten existed until his message appeared. I'd logged in to delete the account, scatter the photos like ashes, when his words popped up again. He'd asked one question: "If you were to describe yourself with one word, three syllables, what would it be?"

It stopped me. Most men led with "Hey, beautiful." But this required thought. I stared at the screen, then typed: "Butterfly."

"Why?" He wrote back.

"Because a butterfly starts off ugly," I answered. "It struggles. But in the end, it becomes something beautiful—distinctive, unlike anything else." We exchanged numbers, and I deleted the app that same night.

And just like that, there he was: Kevin. Brown-haired, blue-eyed, and so Midwestern it ached—Kevin wore Clarks shoes, khakis that never wrinkled, and believed hot sauce belonged on everything, including, God help me, pancakes. A white guy who lived in Arizona, spoke in full sentences like punctuation was a moral obligation, and held doors open for strangers as if democracy depended on it. If I had a type, it definitely wasn't him.

But he had this quiet way of being steady. Funny without trying. Patient in a way that made me narrow my eyes at first. *What's your game, mister?* Spoiler: His game was patience, showing up, and staying.

The Dinner Test

The moment he stayed for dinner, my father didn't wait for the first bite. "I'll be honest," Papi said, ignoring Mami's sharp kick under the table, "my daughter isn't easy. She's stubborn as a mule and won't tolerate disrespect. Are you sure you can handle that?"

Kevin didn't flinch. He adjusted in his chair, the wood groaning beneath him like an old tree bending in the wind. "Sir," he said, locking eyes with my father, "I don't want easy. I want her to be real with me. Your daughter's fire is why I love her—and I plan to spend my life earning the honor of standing beside it." Mami stopped kicking. Papi's frown softened, just a little.

The Proposal

Three months after our first date, he asked. Four months later, we married.

We had planned a picnic in Central Park that day in May. The sun hung golden in the sky, dappling light through the new spring leaves as we walked. Something was off—Kevin's hands were sweaty, his breathing uneven.

"Are you okay?" I asked for the third time. "You look pale."

"I feel amazing," he said, but his voice trembled.

When we reached the bridge, he stopped suddenly. The world seemed to pause with him. His hands shook as he turned to me, his blue eyes brighter than I'd ever seen them.

"I've never felt this kind of connection before," he said. "You're my best friend. I don't ever want to lose you." Then he was on one knee, a velvet box appearing in his palm like magic. "Will you be in my life forever? Will you marry me?"

The ring caught the sunlight, scattering prismatic sparks across the wooden planks beneath us. I couldn't breathe. Couldn't speak. My hands flew to my mouth as tears blurred my vision.

"Is that a yes?" his voice cracked on the last word.

"Yes!" The word burst from me like a dam breaking.

He slid the ring onto my finger, his hands steadier now, as if this single act was the most natural thing in the world. Four months later, we married.

The Doubters

My mother called the morning of our wedding. "Are you sure?" she asked, for the hundredth time. "You barely know him. Marriage is hard enough when you know the person—how can you build a life with a stranger?"

I understood her fear. Kevin had proposed after three months, and we were getting married only four months later. To everyone watching, it looked reckless—like grief had sanded down my common sense.

But here's what they didn't see:

The way he memorized how I took my coffee (three extra shots of espresso, no sugar with caramel macchiato creamer). How he'd drive forty minutes at midnight because I mentioned craving a Philly Cheesesteak. When I woke up gasping from nightmares from upcoming premonitions, he didn't try to fix it—just pulled me closer and whispered "I'm here" into my hair until my heartbeat matched his.

Mom wasn't wrong—marriage *is* hard. But sometimes you recognize a person's soul faster than their habits.

And with Kevin, for the first time, the dead woman singing off-key in our kitchen became a shared joke, not a secret. Spirits interrupting intimacy led to laughter, not apologies. My rejection of corporate life wasn't a failure—it was freedom.

My parents mourned the traditional milestones I was abandoning. They couldn't understand that in Kevin's arms, I wasn't losing myself. I was finally whole.

Kevin's Wisdom

One night, after a fight where I braced for frustration, he cupped my face and said, "You're not a problem to solve, Cyn. You're a person to love." And for the first time, I believed it.

Marriage Tip:

Find someone who loves you enough to put up with your OCD but isn't afraid to leave socks on the floor just to watch you twitch. Kevin didn't try to fix me. He didn't get scared when I told him about the spirits. He didn't run when I told him about the miscarriages, or the grief, or the parts of me that still belonged to people who were no longer here. He just held my hand literally, figuratively, always.

Maybe that's what love is. Not the grand gestures or the movie moments, but the quiet, consistent presence of someone who sees all of you—the messy, the magical, the broken, the haunted—and says, "I'll stay."

Marrying Kevin didn't silence the ghosts or erase the grief. But it gave me something new: a witness. A partner. A sense that maybe this world—*this life*—was worth staying in, too.

Because love, real love, doesn't rescue you from the fire. It sits beside you in the flames.

Chapter 9: The Mountains Call

New York has a rhythm all its own; fast, loud, relentless. It pulses under your skin, fuels your fire, and tests your patience every time a cab nearly kills you crossing Broadway. For years, that noise was my heartbeat. The city raised me, scarred me, toughened me. It taught me to survive. But survival isn't peace. I didn't know I needed stillness until the mountains called.

Dream Lake, Colorado. Ten thousand feet above sea level, where the air thins out and so does the noise in your head. The first time I stood at the edge of that lake, I swear the world stopped spinning. There were no horns, no subways, no spirits whispering from cracked brownstones. Just silence—and wind that felt like it was scrubbing my soul clean.

Up there, grief feels smaller. It's not gone, but less sharp, less all-consuming. At that altitude, even the ghosts seem tired. Or maybe they just respect the quiet.

Hiking Revelation:
Life isn't about reaching the summit, it's not about racing to the top, nor is it about face-planting on the way up. Life is about never giving up. It's

about moving forward while valuing every step. Rushing blinds you. It steals the moment that matters: the sun warming your kin, the wind whispering through the trees, the way your breath syncs with the earth's rhythm. When you hurry, you miss the messages hidden in the journey. But when you slow down, you see things from a new perspective. You learn patience. And if you're patient, you won't miss the opportunities that arise, because life's greatest lessons aren't waiting at the top; they're scattered along the path, waiting for you to notice.

I've never been what you'd call "outdoorsy." My idea of nature used to be a fire escape with a potted plant. But something about the mountains disarmed me. Maybe it was oxygen deprivation. Or maybe it was the humbling reminder that I am tiny in the face of something ancient and sacred.

I remember sitting on a sun-warmed rock, sweat-soaked and gasping, when I felt it: *stillness*. Not silence as the absence of sound, but the presence of peace. That rare, holy silence that says, *You can stop running now. You're safe here.*

That's what the mountains gave me—a place to rest. A place where I didn't have to be the strong one, or the haunted one, or the one holding everyone else's pain. I could just be *Cynthia*. No expectations, no ghosts, no checklists. Just a woman breathing in thin air, letting go, little by little, with every step. And in that release, I found something unexpected: *I found Myself.*

Photo Tip:
The best shots come at the golden hour, when the light makes even our scars look soft.

Chapter 10: Cooking with Family

Baking My Way to Peace

Grief is sticky as caramel. I baked it into *tres leches* cakes and brownies. My kitchen became my confessional.

In our family, food isn't just sustenance—it's therapy, tradition, and performance art. A pot simmering on the stove is a confession booth. A shared meal is a ceasefire, and no one commands the kitchen stage quite like Títi Millie. She moves with the precision of a conductor, her wooden spoon a baton orchestrating garlic, onion, and the golden glow of *achiote*. Her *arroz con salchicha* isn't just a dish-it's a sacrament. The way she coaxes the rice into fluffy perfection, the way the salty-sweet bite of the sausages makes everyone's shoulders drop in surrender. She treats the stove like a sacred altar, and we, her devoted congregation, line up with paper plates held like offering trays.

Decades later, it's still true. The kitchen fills with the same smells, the same laughter, the same unspoken rule: No one touches the pot until Titi gives the signal. And when she finally lifts the lid, steam resigns like a blessing, we all remember—this is how love tastes.

Uncle Jr's *pernil*? Legendary. Dangerous, even. Títi Mayra's beans ... yummy. Dinelia's potato salad is to die for.

Cooking with them was never about the recipes; it was about stories. About passing down unwritten family lore through *sofrito*-stained fingers and laughter loud enough to rattle the saucepans. It was about learning how to smash garlic, while hearing old tales of Puerto Rico, hurricanes and heartbreak, and survival.

Cooking together became our ritual. Our way of being close without saying too much. Our family men aren't known for their emotional vulnerability—but they will tell you they love you through an extra scoop of *arroz con gandules*.

In that kitchen—whether it was Abuela's with her freshly picked peas simmering or Titi Millie's with its symphony of bubbling pots—I learned the alchemy of belonging. The difference between *sofrito* and love—none. Between simmering and stewing—one's culinary, and the other emotional. That a pinch of salt can save a dish, but silence can't save a family.

Mostly, I learned that healing isn't a single ingredient. It's the slow accumulation, the way garlic softens in oil, the way time softens memories. It's what happens when a pot's been stirred by three generations of hands: your great-grandmother's knuckles, thickened from kneading; your mother's wrist, flicking cumin into broth like she's throwing a wish in a well; your fingers, now learning the weight of the ladle and the weight of legacy. We don't just cook to eat. We cook to remember who we've been, and to decide who we'll become.

Family recipes, like family secrets, are passed down with caution. Someone always gets burned. But when done right, they feed more than your belly; they feed your spirit.

So now, when the world feels too much, I find myself in my kitchen, channeling my aunt and uncle—talking to the pork, tasting the rice like a judge on a *telenovela*, and knowing deep in my soul: this is how we remember who we are. One sofrito-stained spoon at a time.

Recipe hint: Cynthia's 'You'll Be Alright' Sweet Cakes—always add extra lemons. Always.

My family's Puerto Rican *Sofrito* Recipe:
Sofrito is a base used in traditional Hispanic cooking for stews, beans, and meat.

Ingredients
- 5 green peppers seeded and chopped
- 2 red peppers seeded and chopped
- 4 cubanelle peppers seeded and chopped
- 1 pack or about 12 aji dulce peppers, seeded and chopped
- 5 cups Spanish onions chopped

- 1 cup of chopped garlic
- 1 bunch of *recao* chopped (culantro, also known as Eryngium Foetidum, is also known as Saw Leaf Herb). Culantro is not the same as cilantro. Culantro is a distinct herb with a pungent, earthy flavor much stronger than cilantro.
- 1 bunch of cilantro chopped (Coriander)
- 1/4 cup of vinegar

Instructions
- Once everything has been rinsed and seeded, in small batches, blend them in either a food processor or blender. I always start with the onions on the bottom because they release liquid, which makes blending the herbs easier. Store some in a mason jar and freeze the rest.

Traditional Puerto Rican *arroz con gandules* recipe
Puerto Rican Rice with Pigeon Peas

Ingredients:

- 2 cups long-grain white rice (or Carolina rice) washed until water is clear, then strain
- 1 can (15 oz) *gandules* (pigeon peas), drained (or fresh if available)
- 3 cups water or chicken broth (for richer flavor)
- ¼ cup *sofrito* (homemade is best—see recipe)
- 2 tbsp *achiote* oil (or olive oil + 1 tbsp annatto seeds)
- 1 small ham steak or ½ cup diced *tocino* (salt pork), chopped
- 1 tsp ground cumin
- 1 tsp dried oregano
- 1 packet of *cubitos en polvo (caldo de pollo),* a dry packet of concentrated broth powder.
- 3 garlic cloves chopped, mashed
- 15 stems of cilantro chopped
- 1 packet (2 tsp) *Sazón con culantro y achiote*
- 1 bay leaf
- ½ cup pitted green olives (optional, we always add it)

Instructions:

1. Infuse the Oil:

- Heat *achiote* oil (or make your own by warming olive oil + annatto seeds for 2 mins, then strain).

- Sauté ham/*tocino* until crispy. Remove some for garnish if desired.

2. Build the flavor base:

- Lower heat; add *sofrito*, stirring 2-3 mins until fragrant.

- Mix in garlic, cilantro, cumin, oregano, *sazón*, and bay leaf. Let it "dance" (as Títi would say) for 1 minute.

3. Toast the Rice:

- Add washed rice, stirring to coat each grain in the oil and sofrito—toast lightly for 1-2 mins.

4. Simmer & Steam:

- Pour in water/broth, *gandules*, and olives. Stir once, then *DO NOT STIR AGAIN* (this ensures perfect *pegao*—the crispy bottom layer).

- Bring to a boil, then reduce heat to low. Cover tightly. Cook for 25-30 mins until liquid is absorbed.

5. The Grand Finale:

- Remove from heat, fluff rice gently with a fork, and let it rest for 5 mins (like a good story, it needs time to settle).

- Serve with extra crispy ham bits, avocado slices on the side, and sprinkle with lemon or hot sauce.

Lemon Blueberry cake

Ingredients:
- ½ cup (8 Tbsp; 113g) unsalted butter, soften to room temperature
- 1 and ¼ cups (250g) granulated sugar
- ½ cup (100g) packed light brown sugar
- 6 tablespoons (90ml) vegetable oil
- 4 large eggs, at room temperature
- 1 tablespoon pure vanilla extract
- 3 cups (375g) all-purpose flour spooned & leveled
- 2 teaspoons baking powder
- ½ teaspoon baking soda
- ½ teaspoon salt
- 3/4 cup (180ml) buttermilk, at room temperature
- 2-3 tablespoons lemon zest
- ½ cup (120ml) lemon juice (3–4 lemons), at room temperature
- 1 and ½ cups (210g) fresh blueberries (I do not recommend frozen)
- 1 tablespoon all-purpose flour

Cream Cheese Frosting
- 8 ounces (226g) full-fat brick cream cheese, softened to room temperature
- ½ cup (8 Tbsp; 113g) unsalted butter, softened to room temperature

- 3 and ½ cups (420g) confectioners' sugar
- 1 tablespoon (15ml) heavy cream
- 1 teaspoon pure vanilla extract
- Sprinkle some lemon zest as desired (optional)
- A pinch of salt
-

Instructions:

Preheat the oven to 350°F (177°C). Grease three 8-inch cake pans, line with parchment paper rounds, then grease the parchment paper. Parchment paper helps the cakes seamlessly release from the pans.

Make the cake: Using a handheld or stand mixer with a paddle attachment, beat the butter on high until smooth and creamy, about 1 minute. Add granulated and brown sugars and beat on medium-high speed until combined, about 2 minutes. Add the oil and beat until combined and light and creamy, about 3 more minutes. Add the eggs and vanilla and beat on medium speed until everything is completely combined, about 1 minute. Scrape down the sides and bottom of the bowl as needed.

In a large bowl, whisk together the flour, baking powder, baking soda, and salt. Add the dry ingredients to the wet ingredients. Beat on low speed for a few seconds, then beat in the milk, lemon zest, and lemon juice until just combined. Toss the blueberries with 1 tablespoon of flour and gently fold into the batter. The batter is thick. Do not over-mix.

Spoon batter evenly into prepared cake pans. Bake for about 22–26 minutes or until a toothpick inserted in the center comes out clean. Remove from the oven and allow to cool completely in the pan before assembling and frosting.

Make the frosting: Using a handheld or stand mixer with a paddle attachment, beat cream cheese and butter together on medium speed until no lumps remain, about 3 full minutes. Add confectioners' sugar, heavy cream, vanilla extract, and salt with the mixer running on low. Turn the mixer up to high speed and beat for 3 minutes.

Assemble and frost: Refrigerate for at least 45 minutes before cutting or else the cake may fall apart as you cut.

Chapter 11: When Spirits Don't Knock

Not every spirit comes gently. Some crash in like ex-boyfriends with bad timing and no boundaries. Others arrive in whispers, curling into corners of the room like smoke, watching and waiting. Some don't even bother knocking—they just *are*.

There was one night, years ago, when I woke up gasping. Not from a nightmare. Not from a sound. Just a . . . presence. I knew better than to reach for logic, so I reached for my rosary instead.

The air was thick, charged with energy. I could hear my heart pounding louder than the creaks of the old floorboards. And then I felt it—cold, intentional, just behind my right shoulder. I didn't turn around. You never turn around.

Instead, I spoke aloud: *"If you need peace, you're welcome. If you mean harm, you have to go."*

Nothing. No sound. No movement. Just the slow, quiet lift of pressure from the room, as if something had exhaled and left. Some visits are like that. Wordless, but unforgettable.

Being a medium doesn't mean I invite everything in. Boundaries matter—especially with the dead.

I learned that the hard way.

There was a time when I said yes to every spirit. Every whisper in the dark. Every shadow lingering at the edge of my vision. I believed it was my duty—my obligation—to be the bridge, the messenger, the guide. To help the lost cross over. To deliver final words to the living. To ease grief with proof that love outlasts death.

I thought I could carry it all.

But the dead don't always want peace. Some cling to anger, and some don't realize they're gone. And others aren't what they seem.

Now I know: Not every door should be opened. Not every voice deserves an answer.

But some spirits don't want help; they want energy. And if you're not careful, they'll drain you dry—leave you hollowed out—wondering why exhaustion clings to your bones like frost, why your temper flares at nothing, and even why the ivy on your windowsill withers overnight.

I had to learn to protect myself. To smudge the air with sage, to knot prayers into my hair, and to say NO without guilt. Because this gift—this calling—isn't free. You don't just pay in goosebumps and sleepless nights. You pay in pieces. So you learn to choose when to open the door and when to slam it shut.

Occasionally . . . one slips through. Not a shrieking poltergeist or some wailing lost soul. Simply a presence. Quiet, patient, familiar. And you know they didn't wander in by mistake.

The night Julio wouldn't let me ignore him.

I'd sworn off readings at that party. No cards, no whispers, just laughter and bad wine. But spirits don't respect calendars. First, my water glass tipped over. A clean spill, no splash—like an invisible hand nudging it. I dabbed the table silently.

Then a girl—an old friend—slid into the chair beside me. We'd barely hugged before the DJ's track flipped. Her breath caught, "That would've been our wedding song."

I laughed before I could stop myself, "I know."

Her pupils dilated. "How? I never told anyone that."

The name burned my tongue, "Julio's here."

She seized my forearm, nails biting into my skin. And then it poured out of me—his urgency, his warning, "Leave with your mother, not with the others. Not the car."

"Why?" Her voice trembled.

"That's all he's showing me. But he's begging— please."

She left clutching her mom's sleeve, making excuses under the porch light. I watched her taillights vanish, unease slithering down my spine.

Dawn brought the news: A crumpled sedan, no survivors. The exact road she'd have taken.

Julio didn't just slip through that night; he kicked the damn door down.

Today, I still set boundaries, I still say no. But I listen when the quiet ones come knocking.

Chapter 12: The Baby Blanket in the Closet

There's a blanket tucked in the back of my linen closet. Soft, ivory, and grey. Never used. Never washed. Still wrapped in the tissue it came in.

I bought it during my first pregnancy—the one I let myself believe would make it. The one I let myself dream about. I imagined wrapping my baby in that blanket on the way home from the hospital, his tiny face peeking out while I sat in the backseat, watching him breathe.

That moment never came.

Grief is strange. It doesn't ask permission. It lives in the hidden places: the back of a closet, the pause in a song, the smile you fake at baby showers. For years, I couldn't look at that blanket. I couldn't touch it. But I also couldn't throw it away. That would feel like erasing him.

The losses added up. Over time, there were nine more pregnancies. Suffocating heartbreak. My body became a battlefield of hope and disappointment. And every time, the world expected me to bounce back, to keep moving, and be grateful for what I *did* have.

But how do you measure a life that never got

to breathe? How do you grieve someone who only existed in heartbeat monitors and whispered names? Or someone who only lasted a few hours?

Some nights, I would sit in the dark, holding that blanket to my chest like it could bring them back. Like it might absorb my pain and give me something in return. It never did. But it stayed soft.

People said things like, "It just wasn't meant to be," or "God has a plan," or my personal favorite, "At least you know you can get pregnant." As if consolation could be found in the biology of it all.

What they didn't say was, "I see your pain. I see the mother you still are."

Because I am—still. Even without a stroller. Even without midnight feedings. Even without tiny footsteps echoing in the hallway.

Motherhood lives in the phantom weight of arms that remember rocking. In dreams where I braid my daughter's hair with hands that never shook. In the lullabies I hum to no one while washing dishes.

But sometimes—it blooms in visions of my own mother: her hands, older now, cradling a swaddled ghost against her chest. Her laughter rings through a sunlit kitchen that never was, as she lifts a faceless toddler onto hips that never ached from this particular joy.

I am the keeper of a love that outlived their? names. A sculptor of a monument no one else can see.

And when the world looks at me and sees an

empty house—I feel them all; the echo of little hands that never got to hold mine back, the weight of my mother's arms, empty of the grandchildren whose names we never got to whisper into the dark.

The blanket is still there. But now, when I open the closet, I let myself touch it. Not to mourn, but to remember. To honor and to feel. Because love doesn't vanish with a heartbeat, and some babies live forever in the spaces we make for them.

Chapter 13: Ghosts in the Grocery Store

Spirits don't care if you're busy. They don't check your schedule. They don't wait for a full moon or a candlelit séance. Sometimes, they show up while you're reaching for canned beans at the supermarket.

I was in the rice aisle, debating between jasmine and long grain, when I felt the air shift—cold, sharp, familiar. Then I smelled it: my grandfather's aftershave. The same one he used to slap on like holy water before putting on his pressed *guayabera* and fedora.

I turned around. Empty aisle. Then a whisper, *"Tell your mother I said to take care of her front garden and trim the flowers."* He was referring to her house in Puerto Rico.

I froze. I hadn't heard that voice in decades, but there it was—bossy, blunt, and unmistakably *Papi*. I laughed out loud, which of course made the old lady next to me clutch her purse and speed off like I'd threatened her with the ghost of Puerto Ricans past.

That's the thing people don't understand about being a medium—it's not always dramatic. It's not always spooky. Occasionally, it's a simple reminder in the middle of your errands that the people you love never really leave. They just get creative.

I've heard messages while stuck in traffic, folding laundry, even during a pelvic exam (try explaining *that* to your gynecologist). The dead don't wait for you to be in a "spiritual" mood. They just appear—when they need to, how they need to.

And often, it's not even about *you*. It's about the message. You're just the mail carrier.

So, if you ever feel something brush against your shoulder while you're in Target, or you smell your dad's cologne in the detergent aisle, don't panic. Just listen, they're still talking.

Chapter 14: My Mother's Prayers, My Grandmother's Spells

In my family, faith is layered like *arroz con gandules*—Catholicism on top, superstition in the middle, and full-blown *brujería* (witchcraft) at the bottom where the flavor lives.

My grandmother, on the other hand, whispered to herbs and made things disappear. She never used the word witch, but she knew what plants to boil for heartbreak, what oils to rub on your feet when the spirits followed you home, and how to tie a red ribbon around your bedpost to keep the nightmares away.

They believed in God and ghosts, in saints and spirits, in prayer and potion. There was no contradiction—only balance. Heaven handled the big stuff, while the dead handled the personal.

I grew up somewhere between a pew and a spell jar. When I told my mom I could see spirits, she didn't want to hear it. Then I spoke to my grandmother. Abuela didn't flinch. She made me a bath with Florida Water*, sea salt, and basil. "Spirits talk to you," she said, "because you listen. That's a gift, Míja (sweetie), but a gift needs protection."

My mother would take me to her church three days a week—a Christian church—and my father started going to a Catholic church every Sunday. I attended two different churches because my parents thought I needed all the help I could get. Meanwhile, Abuela's spirit taught me how to read energy in candle flames and dreams.

One read the Bible and one burned incense, but they were both trying to keep me safe—in their own languages.

Even now, I still use both. I say the Hail Mary before I open a spiritual channel. I burn sage and palo santo. I keep my grandmother's rosary next to a bowl of water with rosemary and rue. I talk to God, and I talk to my dead.

The Unspoken Pact

As I grew older, so did my mother's understanding. Slowly, warily, she began to accept my gift—not as something holy, but as something mine. We bonded in quiet ways: her hesitant questions, my careful answers. I learned to translate the unseen for her, to soften the edges of what I saw.

And then, one day, she started asking—not just out of fear, but curiosity. "Have you ever seen Abuelo?" she whispered once, her voice thick with hope. I shook my head, and she sighed, disappointed but not surprised. Some doors, it seemed, even the dead kept closed.

We developed an unspoken agreement. She never wanted to know if death was coming for someone she loved—but if I sensed it, I'd find a way to warn her. "Mami, maybe we should visit Tío soon," I'd say lightly, and she'd freeze, just for a second, before nodding. No more words were needed. She'd make the call, we'd go visit, and she would hold his hand a little tighter.

To this day, we still have that pact. She doesn't call my gift a miracle, and she still flinches when I mention a spirit lingering near me. But she no longer fears it. She no longer fears me.

Over time, she's come to understand: I'm not the devil's messenger. I'm not evil. If anything, I'm the opposite—a bridge between what's seen and unseen, trying to bring peace, not panic. My mother may never fully embrace the world I walk in, but she no longer prays for me to escape it.

And really, that's the greatest miracle of all.

Protection doesn't always look like armor. Sometimes, it looks like a prayer whispered over boiling water, or a grandmother's hand on your head, telling you to stop doubting what you know.

*Florida Water is a beloved citrus-floral cologne with a refreshing, uplifting scent. For over 200 years, it has been used for spiritual cleansing, purification, and ritual work in traditions like Voodoo, Santería, and *Espiritismo*. Many also use it to honor ancestors, cleanse sacred spaces, or attract positive energy. Its light, versatile scent makes it a staple in both spiritual practice and everyday use.

Common Spiritual Uses:

Cleansing & Protection: Sprinkled in baths, floor washes, or sprayed around rooms to remove negativity.

Ancestor Offerings: Poured as libations or placed on altars to honor spirits.

Energy Boost: Applied to pulse points or used in meditation for clarity and calm.

Key Ingredients: Citrus Oils (orange, lemon, bergamot)—uplifting, purifying.

Floral Notes: Lavender, rose, clove bud—balancing, protective.

Spices: Cinnamon, neroli—warmth, spiritual activation.

I don't separate the sacred from the spiritual anymore. I am both. I come from both. And that's power.

Chapter 15: What the Dead Taught Me About Boundaries

L et me tell you something: the living could stand to take a few notes from the dead when it comes to boundaries.

People assume spirits are intrusive—moaning in corners, moving your keys, showing up in mirrors. And yes, some of them are nosy as hell. But most are polite, they wait, they watch, and they whisper when they feel safe.

The real energy vampires aren't lurking in the shadows—they're the living. For years, I let people pull pieces off me like I was some emotional grab bag. Need advice? I'm there. Want me to drop everything and fix your mess? I'm already in the car. Need to dump your pain into my lap without bothering to ask if I'm okay? Pull up a chair—I've got nowhere left to run.

In the spiritual world, 'vampires' aren't the mythical creatures of folklore. They're the people—or even entities—that feed on your energy, leaving you drained and hollow. These spiritual vampires don't thirst for blood; they crave your vitality, your light, your peace. They come in many forms: the emotional manipulator, the perpetual victim, the one-way street of a friendship where you pour into them but never get filled. Their traits are predictable—drama follows them like a shadow, accountability is a foreign concept, and their needs always seem to eclipse yours.

The worst part? They often don't even realize they're doing it. But ignorance isn't an excuse when you're the one left exhausted, picking up the crumbs of your energy. The dead might haunt, but the living? They'll drain you dry—and still ask for seconds.

Somewhere along the way, I forgot that love isn't supposed to exhaust you. I mistook depletion for devotion, as if suffering was the price of caring. But the dead taught me otherwise.

They don't ask for more than you can give. They don't twist your silence into permission or mistake your softness for surrender. The dead take only what you offer freely—no guilt, no bargaining, no slow bleed of your spirit disguised as connection.

Love shouldn't leave you hollow. And if the living keep demanding what only the dead have earned? Maybe it's time to let the ghosts be your teachers.

When a spirit shows up, the first thing I do is check in with myself: *Am I grounded? Am I protected? Am I willing to receive this message?*

If the answer is no, I light a candle and close the door. No guilt. No explanation. No energetic guilt trip.

Imagine if we did that with people. The dead don't need small talk or politeness. They respect clarity. The living—not so much.

Setting boundaries felt unnatural at first. Like I was breaking some unspoken contract—especially in a culture where women are expected to be available, agreeable, and accommodating. But spirits don't care if you're nice; they care if you're *honest*. They show up when you're authentic, when your energy is clear.

That became my model. I started saying no. Not because I didn't care—but because I *finally* did. About myself, my peace, my energy. I stopped answering texts at midnight. I stopped explaining myself to people who never listened anyway. I started giving myself the same grace I'd always given everyone else.

And guess what? The world didn't end. But the headaches did. There's something powerful about choosing yourself without apology. About understanding that just because someone *needs* you doesn't mean you have to *bleed* for them.

Spirits knock; they wait for permission. I try to do the same now with others, and with myself. Because boundaries aren't barriers. They're sacred. And sometimes, the clearest message from the spirit world is this: You don't owe your energy to everyone who asks for it.

The Power of Letting Go: "It is what it is" isn't surrender; it's defiance. To the guilt, to the ghosts, and to the girl who thought she had to earn her place in this world.

Final Lesson: You don't find yourself. You stop running from yourself.

Chapter 16: I Don't Do Haunted Houses—Because I Live in One

People always assume I love Halloween, haunted houses, ghost tours, and creepy mazes filled with chainsaw noises and fake blood. You know—"fun" scares.

Let me clear something up: If I'm screaming, it's because something real just walked through the wall—not because some guy in a rubber mask jumped out of a fog machine.

I don't do haunted houses, because I *live* in one. When you're a medium, the walls don't keep things out; they keep things in. Energy settles in corners. Memories echo in the baseboards. You don't get to choose who visits, only how you respond.

I once had to pause making *arroz con gandules* because there was a Civil War soldier pacing my hallway. Another time, I was brushing my teeth and saw a woman behind me in the mirror, adjusting her pearls like it was 1947.

You learn to adapt. You also learn the difference between a spirit and a mood. Because some energies aren't people—they're *leftovers*. Residue. Emotion that stains the air like smoke. Grief so heavy it clings to the drapes. Anger so sharp it makes your electronics go haywire.

My house has been staged more times than a yoga studio. I've got crystals by the doors, bowls of salt under the bed, and Florida Water in a spray bottle like it's Febreze. People come over and ask why it smells like a botanical garden had a nervous breakdown. I just smile. *Welcome to my sanctuary.*

Don't mistake sacred for peaceful. This home holds stories, some loud, some quiet. I've had dreams here that weren't mine. I heard laughter in empty rooms. Once, I found my grandmother's rosary on the kitchen floor—three years after I lost it.

I'm not scared, not anymore. You learn who means harm and who just wants to be seen. I don't always engage, but I always acknowledge, even if it's just a nod. Spirits deserve dignity too.

So no, I don't pay for jump scares or haunted hayrides. Why would I? My everyday life is most people's paranormal.

Chapter 17: Therapy, but Make it Spiritual

You can only hold your breath for so long before your soul starts gasping. That's how I felt walking into my first therapy session—tight-chested, suspicious, and already planning how not to cry. I sat on the couch like it might bite me and asked the therapist, "Ok, how does this work?"

Being a medium, you tend to keep everything to yourself, of course. Because being a medium is lonely, even when you're surrounded by people. You become the keeper of stories, the one others come to for comfort, answers, or closure. But where do *you* go when the grief isn't someone else's? When it's *yours*?

I tried therapy, but I was skeptical, just like most people are skeptical of mediums. I kept it simple, giving her just enough information to help me.

It was more exhausting than anything. The words spilled out, but in the back of my head, a relentless whisper followed: Does she understand? Can she?

I questioned whether she could truly grasp my pain—whether she had ever felt anything like it. Did I just carve open my chest for someone who, despite her degree, might never recognize the shape of my wounds? Therapy was supposed to be a relief, but that hour left me hollow, wondering if I'd handed my story to a stranger who could only nod politely from the shore while I drowned.

We unpacked all of it: the losses I had buried beneath jokes, the guilt I'd carried for things no child should carry, and the constant need to earn my worth through service, spiritual or otherwise.

At one point, I said, "I feel like I'm always on call."

She nodded. "So what would it feel like to rest?"

I didn't know. But I wanted to.

Don't get me wrong—I still believe in sage and salt and prayer. But sometimes, what you really need is a professional with a degree and a clipboard, someone who can look you in the eye and say, "That sounds really hard. You don't have to fix it today."

And here's what I learned: you can believe in spirit and still need science, you can talk to your ancestors and still need to unpack your childhood, and you can light candles and still take Zoloft. Healing isn't one-size-fits-all.

Chapter 18: When the Spirits Go Quiet

You'd think I'd miss them—the whispers, the shadows, the flickering lights. But the first time the spirits went quiet—really quiet—I panicked.

No signs. No messages. No chills down my spine in the middle of the night. Just . . . stillness. I checked my altar, refreshed the water, lit new candles, meditated, prayed, and waited.

Nothing.

And then I did the thing I tell everyone *not* to do: I spiraled.

Did I lose my gift? Was I being punished? Was I finally "normal" . . . and if so, why did that feel so awful?

Then I remembered something my grandmother used to say, *"Even the moon rests in darkness."*

Spiritual silence isn't abandonment—it's integration. Sometimes, the spirits step back so *you* can step forward.

The truth is, I had been so busy being a bridge between the worlds that I'd forgotten how to walk on my own. I was burnt out. My energy was scattered. I was tired of holding space for everyone—living or dead.

And so, the quiet came as mercy. That season of silence forced me inward. I read books that had nothing to do with mediumship. I cooked slow meals. I laughed more. I let myself be held by people instead of always being the one doing the holding.

When the spirits eventually returned, it wasn't with a bang. It was a whisper, a dream. A feather on the floor where no bird had been.

They hadn't left me, they'd just waited. Waited for me to remember that I'm not just a messenger. I'm a human being with a heart, with limits, with needs. They helped me learn that sometimes the most spiritual thing you can do is rest. So now, when the silence comes, I welcome it.

It means I've been heard. It means I can exhale. It means I get to be whole again—for myself.

Chapter 19: The Hardest Goodbyes Aren't Always to the Dead

People think the hardest part of being a medium is seeing ghosts. It's not.

It's learning how to say goodbye to the living—the ones who are still breathing, still walking around, but who no longer belong in your story.

Grief isn't reserved for death. You grieve the friend who stopped calling. The sisters who became strangers. The version of yourself you had to outgrow in order to survive.

Letting go of the dead is a sacred act. It's filled with candles and closure, whispered prayers under moonlight, the kind of grief the world understands.

Letting go of the living is messy. It's unanswered texts and aching silence. It's walking away from people who don't get why you're not "fun" anymore. It's saying, I love you, but I love me more.

I used to think love meant forever. Now I know better. Love means presence, respect, and growth. It means recognizing when a connection is holding you back more than it's holding you up.

I had family members who weaponized the word family—toxic, cruel, always ready to blame me for their unhappiness. For years, I took their verbal and emotional abuse, swallowing every hurt because that's what family does, right?

But then I learned: Love shouldn't cost you your peace.

Letting go felt like mourning. I grieved not just the loss of their presence, but the illusion of what I thought family should be. And yet—there was freedom in that grief. I still love them, because they are my blood. But I love myself more. I expect the same respect I give.

When I buried my father, I buried more than just him. I buried the weight of those who mistook my loyalty for weakness. And in that release, I found my own sanity waiting for me.

Some people leave without dying. And that's death, too. In many ways, it's more difficult because there's no funeral. Just distance, space, and a ghost of a memory standing in the doorway of who you used to be with them.

I've had to release people I once swore I'd never live without. Not because I stopped loving them, but because I started loving myself in ways that made their presence feel like poison.

That's the kind of grief no one prepares you for. There's no ritual for it. No flowers, no cards. Just the slow realization that healing sometimes means choosing solitude over chaos, peace over history, and expansion over obligation.

If there's one thing spirits have taught me, it's this: True love doesn't keep you small. It doesn't clip your wings or punish your growth.

The ones meant to walk with you will adjust their pace. The rest? Bless them, release them, and keep walking. Because the road ahead is yours now, and every step forward is a spell of self-return.

Chapter 20: Taming My Inner New Yorker

You can take the girl out of New York, but good luck taking New York out of the girl. The city's grit never leaves you. These days, when my OCD demands order or my grief feels too heavy, I hear my father's voice in the wind: "*Dale* (go ahead), Cindy. It is what it is." For the first time, I believed him.

My inner New Yorker still shows up uninvited. She's loud, she's impatient, she argues with Siri, talks with her hands, and firmly believes everyone's walking too slowly. She doesn't *ask* for space—she takes it. And don't even get her started on bad bagels or weak coffee.

But here's the thing I've come to understand: She was born from survival. She kept me sharp when I needed to be. She protected me when I didn't know how to ask for protection, and she made sure I was never small, never swallowed, never invisible.

I used to resent her—the edge, the walls, the need to be *ready for anything.* But now I see her differently. My inner New Yorker is part of my magic. She's the grit beneath the grace. The fire in the ritual. The voice that says, *No, that's not okay,* even when everyone else stays quiet.

She's also tired sometimes, and for the first time in my life, I let her rest. I'm baking now. I sit in silence without needing to fill it. I walk more slowly. I let things be. I know the difference between urgency and importance.

I still talk to spirits, and I still talk to myself. But now, I also listen.

Grief, love, and healing aren't linear; they swirl and circle back. They whisper in the wind when you least expect it. But I've learned to welcome the mess. To let the past inform me but not define me. To let the spirits guide me, but not carry me.

To let the New Yorker in me soften—without ever disappearing. I'm not fully healed—I don't want to be. Healing is a rhythm, not a finish line.

But I am whole and that's enough. Because somewhere between the ghosts and the grief, the city and the silence, the love I lost and the love I found again—I finally came home to myself.

Cynthia Barris

Epilogue:

A Letter to My 16-Year-Old Self

"You will lose. You will break.
And you will rise—not in spite of it, but because of it.
Also, pluck your eyebrows.
Trust me."

About the Author

Cynthia Barris was born in Manhattan, NY, and spent much of her adolescence in New York City and New Jersey. Later in life, Cynthia pursued her Bachelor of Science in Business Administration from Becker College. After spending 17 years as a Medical Financial Specialist in the corporate world, she transitioned to a nonprofit organization in Upstate New York, where she helped provide employment opportunities for individuals with disabilities.

Seeking a life of adventure and fulfillment, Cynthia and her husband, Kevin, sold their home in Upstate New York to travel across the USA, discovering peace and happiness along the way. During her journeys, she reignited her passion for writing and photography, capturing the beauty of her experiences on her YouTube channel, @TheSlomovement.

The majestic landscapes of South Dakota and Colorado's mountains have become Cynthia's greatest inspiration, offering both creative fuel and serenity. Through her writing, she shares her transformative journey, encouraging others to embrace life's unexpected paths. Follow Cynthia's adventures and literary work as she continues to explore, create, and inspire.

Exorcising My Inner New Yorker